KPO BTS QUIZ BOOK

123 Fun Facts Trivia Questions About K-Pop's Hottest Band

Ordering Information: Quantity sales. Special discounts are available on quantity purchases by corporations, associations, and others. For details, contact the publisher at the email address above.

Printed in the United States of America

ISBN-13: 979-11-88195-35-0

www.newampersand.com

14 13 12 11 10 / 10 9 8 7 6 5 4 3 2 1

Q: 001

In 2017, BTS made their first US TV debut
on which show...?

A: American Music Awards 2017

Q: 002

Which title did BTS perform on their US TV debut?

A: "DNA"

Q: 003

On November 27, 2017, BTS appeared on THIS famous US TV talk show, performing "Mic Drop" and "DNA"

A: The Ellen DeGeneres Show

Q: 004

THIS title track released in February of 2017 crashed the Melon digital chart upon its initial release due to traffic overload.

A: "Spring Day (봄날)"

Q: 005

True or False...?

On May 21, BTS won the Top Social Artist Award at the Billboard Music Awards, becoming the second Korean group to win a BBMA, after PSY.

A: False - BTS was the first

Q: 006

On the November 22, BTS was announced to be officially recognized by THIS organization as a musical group with the most Twitter engagement.

A: The Guinness World Record Book for 2018

Q: 007

On June 12, 2013, BTS debuted with THIS song...

A: "No More Dream"

Q: 008

Their second full album, Wings (2016), peaked at THIS RANK on the Billboard 200, which marked the highest chart ranking for a K-pop album ever.

A: 26

Q: 009

BTS group also managed to debut on the Billboard Hot 100 for the first time with THIS SONG, which entered at #85 and peaked at #67.

A: "DNA"

Q: 010

On the very first Episode of *American Hustle Life*,
BTS travels to THIS CITY to learn Hip Hop.

 **A:** Los Angeles

Q: 011

THIS member was a film arts student at Konkuk University before being streetcast for auditions.

A: Jin

Q: 012

THIS member was an underground rapper in Daegu.

A: Suga

Q: 013

THIS member was part of a street dance team named Neuron, and was active in the underground dancing scene.

A: J-Hope

Q: 014

THIS member enrolled in Busan High School of Arts as the top student in modern dance, but later transferred to Korea Arts High School with V, who auditioned in Daegu.

A: Jimin

Q: 015

Jungkook was cast by seven agencies after auditioning for Superstar K, but eventually chose Big Hit, reportedly after watching THIS member rap.

A: Rap Monster

Q: 016

In 2013, BTS starred their own variety show by SBS-MTV, titled...?

A: Rookie King Channel Bangtan

Q: 017

BTS' first concert was titled...?

A: 2014 BTS Live Trilogy – Episode II: The Red Bullet

Q: 18

During 2014 Mnet Asian Music Awards, BTS had a collaboration stage with THIS K-Pop group.

A: Block B

Q: 019

In 2015, BTS toured THIS country for the first time with the Wake Up: Open Your Eyes tour.

A:
Japan - They performed to 25,000 fans in Tokyo, Osaka, Nagoya and Fukuoka.

Q: 020

On May 5, 2015, THIS song won first place on SBS MTV's The Show, which marked their first ever music show win since their debut.

A: "I Need U"

Q: 021

In 2015, BTS donated 7 tons (7,187 kg) of THIS to charity at the K-Star Road opening ceremony held in Apgujeong-dong.

A: Rice

Q: 022

True or False...?
In 2016, Nexon released character avatars based on the members for their RPG game Elsword.

A: True

Q: 023

"Spring Day" was produced by which BTS member?

A: Rap Mosnter

Q: 024

Who belong to the maknae line in BTS?

A: Jimin, V, Jungkook

Q: 025

True or False...?
BTS' motto is 'To stop the suppression and prejudice and to defend our music and generation.'

A: True - Hence the name 'Bullet Proof'

Q: 026

BTS dorm has a set of strictly enforced rules. If a member breaks the rule, they have to...?

A: Pay 1,000 Korean Won

Q: 027

THIS legendary Hip Hop musician commented about BTS Track Cypher Pt2: Triptych on Twitter, saying "Tell them keep on writing and reciting!!!! Good work!!! Nice!!! They sound very confident and precise! Love it!"

A: DMC Darryl

Q: 028

BTS' own TV channel on YouTube is called...?

A: BANGTAN TV

Q: 029

The dance moves for Boy in Luv are better known as...?

A: "King Kong Dance" and "Shaving Dance"

Q: 030

True or False...?
BTS had their version of 'Harlem Shake' dance video.

A: True - it's on YouTube

Q: 031

Which BTS member said... "It's so loud. I'm gonna die. These guys.. ah.. These guys are not normal." on M! Countdown Begins on 09.25.2014?

A: Jin

Q: 032

Jin's favorite color is...?

A: Pink

Q: 033

Jin has a habit of doing THIS when hungry.

A: Blinking his left eye

Q: 034

When Jin made THIS for J-Hope and it tasted really good, and it made J-Hope speechless because he thought it tasted as good as what his mom's made.

A: *Miyeok Guk* (seaweed soup)

Q: 035

True or False...?
Jin thinks Super Mario characters and the monsters in
Maple Story are very ugly.

A: 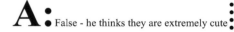 False - he thinks they are extremely cute

Q: 036

Jin made a huge mistake during their first performance at M! Countdown. What happened?

A: His pants went down all the way to his thighs.

Q: 037

Besides "Bangtan Sonyeondan" or "Bulletproof Boy Scouts", BTS also stands for...?

A: "Beyond The Scene"- in 2017, BTS announced that they will include "Beyond The Scene" as their new brand identity.

Q: 038

True or False...?
BTS was the most liked artist on Facebook in March 2016.

A:
False - BTS was the most retweeted artist on Twitter in March 2016.

Q: 039

True or False?
Twitter launched its first ever K-pop emoji featuring BTS.

A: True

Q: 040

In June 2017, THIS magazine named BTS as one of the 25 most influential people on the internet.

A: Time Magazine

Q: 041

Before debuting in 2013, THIS BTS member was already performing as an underground rapper!

A:

Rap Monster (he had released several tracks informally, including a collaboration with Zico)

Q: 042

THIS BTS member was originally cast by seven agencies after leaving auditions for "Superstar K".

A: Jungkook - but eventually chose Big Hit Entertainment

Q: 043

What as the name of BTS' first debut album?

A: School Trilogy

Q: 044

THIS BTS member played saxophone for over 3 years.

A: v

Q: 045

THIS BTS member said that he would beat up
any member who damages his beloved toys!

A:

Q: 046

BTS' fandom name is...?

A: A.R.M.Y ("Adorable Representative M.C. for Youth")

Q: 047

Suga is the stage name for which BTS member?

A: Yoongi

Q: 048

True or False...?
Jimin's stage name was supposed to be either
'Baby J' or 'Young Kid'

A: True

Q: 049

Before Jimin started listening to Hip Hop, he only listened to THIS music.

A: Classical Music

Q: 050

Which BTS member takes the most time to take a shower?

A: Jungkook

Q: 051

True or False...?
J-Hope is a gym rat, as he spends most of his free time working out.

A: False - J-Hope said he hates exercising.

Q: 052

BTS chose THIS K-KPOP group as their role model.

A: Big Bang

Q: 053

True or False...?
All BTS members come from the same region - Jejudo

A: False - They all come from different provinces

Q: 054

THIS BTS member thinks his legs are beautiful as those of
Girls' Generations'.

A: Suga

Q: 055

Whenever V has a problem, he would go to THIS BTS member.

A: Jimin (they are the same age)

Q: 056

A: Jimin

THIS BTS member is know for having no *aegyo*.

Q: 057

Before debut, THIS BTS member already had several
tracks released as an underground artist, including a
collaboration with Zico.

A: Rap Monster

Q: 058

THESE TWO BTS members always go to the gym together.

A: Jin and Jimin

Q: 059

True or False...?
Jin is the member who usually messes up the dorm.

A: False - he is the one who usually CLEANS up the dorm.

Q: 060

Jin wears really strong prescription glasses but he doesn't like wearing them because...

A: That makes him feel insecure.

Q: 061

True or False...?
Jin's nickname is "Jin Prince" and "Pink Prince"

A: False - "Jin Princess" and "Pink Princess"

Q: 062

Jin's favorite song at Karaoke is...

A: "This Song" by 2AM

Q: 063

Jin said that if he could get a day off, he'd like to have THIS member as a servant.

A: Suga

Q: 064

True or False...?
Jin's favorite movies genre is horror movies.

A: 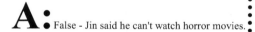 False - Jin said he can't watch horror movies.

Q: 065

When Jin was younger, he wanted to become...

A: A detective

Q: 066

SUGA is known as THIS of BTS because he's in charge of fixing things that other members breaks, and also does maintenance work such as changing the light bulbs and fixing the toilet.

A: Father

Q: 067

SUGA was inspired to rap after listening to THIS song and decided to pursue a career in music after listening to THIS song.

A: "Fly" by Epik High / "Ragga Muffin" by Stony Skunk

Q: 068

True or False...?
Suga was a name given by the CEO Bang Sihyuk
because he loves desserts.

A: False - because he has a pale complexion and his smile is sweet.

Q: 069

Whenever Suga is in trouble or has concerns, he will talk to THIS member because they are of similar age and also have a lot of things in common.

A: Rap Monster

Q: 070

When Suga gets nervous, he talks in...

A: Satoori (dialect)

Q: 071

True or False...?
It took Suga over a year to write the song
'좋아요' (Like It).

A: False - Took him just under 40 minutes. (In middle school he learned classical composition and started writing songs daily after that.)

Q: 072

There is one thing Suga wants to steal from Jungkook because it can't even be bought with money. What is it?

A: His age

Q: 073

According to V, Suga is a fantastic cook and he makes THIS, which is really out of this world.

A: Kimchi Fried Rice

Q: 074

When Suga was asked who to bring along with him if he were stranded on a deserted island, he picked THIS member.

A: Jimin - Because Suga doesn't talk a lot, and he is not the fun type, but Jimin is pleasant and mature.

Q: 075

Before debut, J-Hope hated doing THIS but now
he changed his mind for his fans.

A: Aegyo

Q: 076

J-Hope and THIS B.A.P member audition together for their JYP audition.

A: Youngjae

Q: 077

V once said J-Hope is like THIS animation character,
because he always find the solution.

A: Doraemon

Q: 078

J-Hope said that the kind of super power he would like to have is...?

A: Mind reading so he can know the truth.

Q: 079

Jin once said about J-Hope that he is like THIS animal because at home he's really untidy and leaves things scattered around and likes to clinging to people around him all the time."

A: Beagle Puppy

Q: 080

Things J-Hope wants to steal from other members is
Rap Monster's rap skills and his good English, and Jimin's
THIS.

A: Chocolate Abs

Q: 081

One of Rap Monster's many nicknames was THIS - He was so bad at dancing so his dance teacher and the company staff called him that as a tongue in cheek remark.

A: 'Dance Prodigy'

Q: 082

Rap Monster once said that he is fire whereas THIS member is water - he's good at 'turning off' his bad habits, and is really sociable so he's good at blending in.

A: J-Hope

Q: 083

True or False...?
Rap Monster wrote the lyrics of "No More Dream"
because he had no dream when he was in school.

A: True

Q: 084

Before debut, Rap Monster was active in underground hip-hop scene. His stage name was...?

A: Runcha Randa

Q: 085

When Jimin was asked to describe and compare Rap Monster to something other than a human, he said Rap Monster is like...

A:

A Lion because even if he gets caught, he would break everything and escape.

Q: 086

In the dorm, Rap Monster is in charge of doing THIS.

A: Sweeping the floor.

Q: 087

Rap Monster has a dog named...

A: Rap Mon

Q: 088

Rap Monster's favorite girl artist is THIS because he thinks she has a deep voice and he likes all the songs from her.

A: Younha

Q: 089

Jimin generally solves his problems himself, but if he can't, he will share with THIS member.

A: v

Q: 090

Jimin said that if he had a super power, he'd like to...

A: Be able to talk to animals.

Q: 091

For Halloween, Jimin said he wants to wear
THIS costume.

A: Dionsaur

Q: 092

Jimin said that things he want to steal from other members
is Rap Monster's height, V's talents, J-Hope's cleanliness,
and Suga's THIS.

A: Diverse knowledge

Q: 093

Jimin favourite song at karaoke is THIS
because in the past he had an unrequited love.

A: Taeyang "Naman Barabwa" (Only Look At Me)

Q: 094

When asked what he'd do if he got a day off, Jimin jokingly wants to go on a date with THIS BTS member, holding hands together.

A: Jungkook

Q: 095

For Jimin, THIS is his life. When dancing in the practice room without THIS, he feels he can't make strong expressions and he will likely get shy.

A: Eyeliner

Q: 096

According to Jimin, the noisest member of BTS is...?

A: 1st - V, 2nd - Jungkook, 3rd - Jimin

Q: 097

THIS BTS member was chosen as the weirdest member of the group because he has a 4D personality.

A:

Q: 098

V played the saxophone for 3 years since 7th grade and then stopped in this fourth year. He once received an award after playing THIS SONG.

A: "Desperado" by the Eagles

Q: 099

V describes himself as THIS animal.

A: Monkey - When he was little, he got spit on by a chimpanzee at the zoo and after that incident his friends started saying that he is a chimpanzee's rival, monkey.

Q: 100

True or False...?
All member said, V is the most member
who has a lot of girl fans.

A: True

Q: 101

During 'Jump Rope Challenge' on MBC's *Show Champion*, V's pants kept coming down, but he didn't give up and kept jumping - getting the highest score by jumping HOW MANY times?

A: 120

Q: 102

When V celebrated his Birthday (2013.12.30 at MBC *Gayo Daejun*), he shared birthday with THIS famous singer. He said to V "Hey, is it your Birthday today? It's mine too! Let's blow the candle together."

A: K. Will

Q: 103

If V gets a day off, he would like to...

A: See his parents

Q: 104

Interestingly, V said he doesn't like wearing THESE.

A: Shoes

Q: 105

V and J-Hope did Self PR Time mission at
M!Countdown Begins (2014.09.18). What did V do?

A:
He roared like a lion in the MGM trade mark at the beginning of their movies.
In the end, V said 'bye' with the weirdest expression.

Q: 106

True or False...?
The reason Jungkook went to the U.S. is to learn dancing.

A: True - Jungkook auditoned at Mnet's Superstar K2 and got cast there. When he danced, CEO Bang Sihyuk told him,"No emotion. No emotion while dancing."

Q: 107

Which of the following ISN'T
Jungkook's many nicknames...?
1. Jeon Jungkookie 2. Golden Maknae 3. Frog 4. Kookie

A: 3. Frog

Q: 108

True or False...?
Jungkook's dream when he was little is to become a
badminton player, but changed his mind after listening
to...

A:  A G-Dragon's song

Q: 109

Jungkook really wants to learn is THIS. He studies it really hard because he wants to be a musician who writes brilliant lyrics like his hyungs.

A: Composing

Q: 110

Jungkook said one thing he wants to steal from Jimin is...?

A: 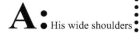 His wide shoulders

Q: 111

Jungkook said that he is addcited to THIS recently.

A: 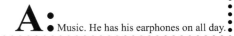 Music. He has his earphones on all day.

Q: 112

When asked who he would choose as a duet partner, Jungkook chose THIS girl singer.

A: IU

Q: 113

Jungkook once said "I suddenly have a lot of wrinkles near my eyes…" and he said THIS would be the likely culprit!

A: Smiling a lot.

Q: 114

Jungkook is good at drawing - and he thinks it is easiest to draw THIS member wearing sunglasses with wavy hair.

A:

Q: 115

Jungkook said the body parts which he feels
most confident with are...?

A: Thighs and lips

Q: 116

True or False...?
Jungkook's ideal type of girl who wears
a boxy, white button up shirt.

A: True

Q: 117

THIS member has performed on MBC *Music Core* a few times before, rapping for Jo Kwon of 2AM during his "I'M DA ONE" solo promotions. He was the main feature in the track "Animal".

A: J-Hope

Q: 118

On November 7, 2017, Big Hit Entertainment confirmed a collaboration with THESE DJ's for a remix of "Mic Drop" released on November 24.

A: Steve Aoki and Desiigner

Q: 119

True or False...?

On December 1, BTS won their third Daesang, Artist of the Year, at the 2017 MAMA. By doing this, BTS became the second K-pop artist to win the award two years in a row, after Big Bang.

A: False - they were the first ever.

Q: 120

BTS's first Japanese studio album was titled...?

A: Wake Up

Q: 121

True or False...?
Rap Monster strongly supports LGBT.

A:

Q: 122

THIS member has a very interesting sleeping habits - He screams, yells, talks, kicks, and even asks other members to get stuff for him.

A: v

Q: 123

Jimin's ideal type of girl is someone who's nice, cute, charming, and MUST be THIS than him!

A: shorter

Printed in Great
Britain
by Amazon